STEVEN SCHOOL

Tools Of The Trade

Secrets of book promotion

STEVEN SCHOOL

STEVEN SCHOOL

Copyright © 2013 Steven School

All rights reserved.

ISBN:1494819465
ISBN-13:9781494819460

STEVEN SCHOOL

DEDICATION

It was my dream to become a writer. It was not easy at first but I found my way. I discovered by practical experience that publishing a book, is only half of the battle, now one must learn the art of promotion which can appear a daunting task, here in this book, I have shared with you my own secret strategy which has increased my sales exponentially and without incurring great expense.

STEVEN SCHOOL

STEVEN SCHOOL

CONTENTS

Secrets Of Book Promotion

STEVEN SCHOOL

STEVEN SCHOOL

ACKNOWLEDGMENTS

I would like to acknowledge amazon for giving me the opportunity to make my dream a reality.

STEVEN SCHOOL

STEVEN SCHOOL

SECRETS OF BOOK PROMOTION

PROVERBS 3:16

Blessed is he who finds wisdom
For she is more precious than jewels
And nothing you desire compares with her
Long life is in her right hand
In her left hand are riches and honor
All her ways are pleasant
And all her paths are peace

DECIDE WHO YOU WANT TO BE.

Have you ever noticed that some people are rich and some people are poor?, have you wondered what some of the differences are between the two?, it could sometimes be that some were born with the proverbial silver spoon while others were not, however there is one major difference that I have noticed between the two classes and that is mindset.

People have the ability to choose who they want to be, many persons design their life to be poor, by creating debt, and by spending more than they earn. Debt compounds interest, late fees, and penalties.

Want to buy something but don't have the money?, hey! Finance it! Pretty soon we wake up one day and realize that we owe a ton of money to someone else and that a large portion of the payments that we make simply go to interest which continues to compound and the debt simply gets bigger and bigger. Whose choice was it to create this? Could we have done something differently? If we learned to design our life to create debt, can we learn to redesign our mindset to create wealth?

I was this person at one time, it took years for me to simply understand and realize that all I had to do was to flip the switch from negative to positive. I completely redesigned my life so that my actions eliminate debt and build income.

The first step that I took was to stop incurring debt, then I worked at getting everything paid off, I do not even own a credit card anymore. I also quit paying rent, I scoured through houses for sale in different states that were listed for sale online, until I found one that I could afford to buy, I called the realtor, wrote the check, and moved in. my strategy was that if I didn't have enough money in the bank to purchase this house, then find a cheaper house!

My years of paying excessive rent every month was instantly gone, I used this savings to accrue enough money to purchase a new automobile for cash, no interest, no finance charges, no never ending debt. I redesigned my life to make money, instead of just spending it. One thing that I realized right away is that I need to spend less money than I earn. The excess money that I accrue needs to go to work for me earning interest. Do you choose to spend more than you earn, or do you choose to spend less than you earn?

The type of career that I had chosen for myself many years ago was service plumbing, eventually I realized that I could continue working for someone else which required long hours, nights and weekends, sometimes working seven days per week, and hoping for raises that never came.

And then one day it occurred to me that I could simply learn to "accept the promotion", which means to start my own business, become my own boss, and determine my own rate of pay, as well as set my own hours. So I opened the doors of my new company, my cell phone and service vehicle were my office, I did not need to rent office space or hire employees. I could simply determine the price of each job, make money, and keep it.

I also learned that I can design just about everything that I do to make money for me, any idea that occurs to me, I can create an entire book around and market it.

I recently met with an author friend of mine to discuss book promotional ideas over a cup of coffee at a popular book store, even though we are just friends and it was simply just a business meeting, as we sat there chatting the divine spark of creation illuminated itself in my mind and I began writing a book about this meeting, the book is a fictional romance novel about two people who met in a bookstore.

My favorite pet is the German Rottweiler, because these dogs are very protective of their owners, of course a small dog would also be protective of its owner but not nearly as effective as the Rottie if it becomes needed. These dogs will attack a bear to protect their master, I have actually seen it happen while camping in the mountains and a bear came into our camp to tear up our ice chests, my dog Rudy charged at the bear and drove it away.

Since then, I have always had a great respect for the Rottweiler.

I decided instead of having just one, I might as well become a breeder and let them generate income as well, I now have two females and one male, and they make money.

When I first decided to start writing books I had no idea how or where to start. I had developed an interest in alchemy and began to study it as a hobby, I soon realized that other hobby alchemists had published books about the art. As I wondered how they had managed to do this, I decided to research online how to publish a book. The website that I found was create space and soon I had published my first book.

I quickly realized soon after this, that I was not getting rich overnight with millions of book sales, in fact it took three to four months just to get my first book sale.

My interest in writing books was not over yet, this has become my new hobby and I have already published more than twenty books as well as a few DVD's.

I began to research how to promote a book as well as how to increase book sales and which types of books sell the best. I came across the usual methods posted online by other authors, I also came up with a few ideas of my own. I looked over all of the options that I had unearthed, I then chose the methods that best suited me and infused them together into my own power packed promotional strategy, and then I sat back and watched my sales grow. You will see my techniques in this book and they are all very effective.

Notice at the end of this book, I list the other books that I have published, if this book is available as an electronic ebook (which it is), then the internet search engines can see inside of this book, they will pick up on the keywords, so what does this mean?, it means that if you search for one of my books online, or find it by accident, you are likely to see some of my others books as well, which is the whole point.

You need your book to go viral to get the really big sales, and this means getting it seen and shared by as many people as possible.

So not only does the reader have the option to purchase some of my other books, but by posting them at the end of this book, it will increase the visibility of this book in the search results, and more visibility means more sales.

Have you ever searched online for say, a plumber, pizza, a local restaurant, a casino, an auto mechanic or a myriad of other things and seen a completely unrelated book show up in the search results? If you did, it may be one of mine. Even if you are not looking for my book, my goal is to get it in front of you anyway.

I noticed that there are several self publishing platforms out there, I can create a book at one of them, and then upload it to all of the others, now all of them are promoting and selling my books for me, and not only has this shown a drastic increase in my sales figures, but it was all free, just a simple matter of uploading each one of my books to half a dozen publishers, instead of just one. After doing this, I recently noticed that my books are advertised at many places online, where I did not list them, which is really great in my opinion, two of these companies have actually listed all of my books on ebay, but I didn't have to pay any fees, or take any orders, or make any deliveries, someone else does all that and I just get paid, very nice, I like getting paid while I am sleeping.

Here is a list of the ones that I like,

Createspace
Kindle
Nook
Kobo
Lulu
Smashwords
Ibooks

Many authors have told me to promote my book by creating an ebook version and then giving it away for free, this is complete and utter hogwash, I will happily sell my ebook for 99 cents, and some other authors that I know want anywhere from three to five dollars for their books, but I am happy with my price, of which I usually get anywhere from 35 to 45 cents per sale, it does add up, especially when an ebook can promote my whole series of other books which vary in price. I will sometimes pick a subject and create and ebook just to promote my other books, with this method, instead of paying to promote my products, I am getting paid to promote my own books, and I like that very much.

Now let us move on to free web pages to promote our books, after searching the internet for social media sites and free web pages, I found Wikia. At this site I can create free web pages for all of my books, I can include pictures, links, descriptions, and keywords.

I can put keywords in titles, descriptions, and several other places as well. Did you know that if you are creating a website, when you are choosing background colors and font colors, you can hide additional keywords all over your website, say for example your back ground color is green and you choose the same color font, you can write keywords all over your website which people cannot see, but the search engines can, and they will pick up on these key words and increase your visibility in the search results.

Good Reads, at good reads you can set up your author page, fill out your profile, and network with other authors to help promote each other's book.

I invite authors to my face book friends list so that we can network together to share and promote one another's work, as well as exchange book reviews on amazon, barnes and noble, good reads, and kobo. The more good reviews that you have, the better, if you desire high sales you really need at least 30 good reviews on each book, with an average rating of 3.5 stars or better.

LINKS.

Links and reviews are a gold mine in book promoting, we already covered the reviews and networking with other authors to get that rolling, look me up on face book and you can be part of my network. Now let us advance to links, I like to purchase and review items on amazon.com, and when leaving a review I try to be positive, if I have something negative to say then I usually just won't leave a review at all, Karma. When I select the old review page at amazon it allows me to insert a link to my books in the review, this increases my visibility considerably and it has generated a lot of book sales for me, as well as good reviews on my book. If I write a book on cooking, I might find things on amazon like woks, blenders, pressure cookers, coffee grinders, etc, I will review them, and insert the link to my book. Amazon has created this for us specifically to increase our sales and it works.

Look up your book on amazon, notice the icons there for twitter, pinterest and face book. Use them to share your books with the world, and share them often. The more active that you are on twitter and pinterest, the more followers that you will get, so the more people will see your book. In front of the icons you will see the word share, click on this and you will see the link appear for your book, copy and paste this all over the internet, especially on face book pages.

Would you like to see several social media sites where you can promote your book for free?, simply go to any youtube video, under the video you will see the word share, click on that and about a dozen links will pop up for free social media sites that you can use to promote your products.

On face book I play a game called mafia wars, this attracts a lot of other players to my friends list which means that I have a huge network of face book pages that I can post my books on. Their friends and family can see my books as well as share them. I periodically change my profile picture, I place my book covers here, if you click on the picture to expand then you will also see the link appear along with a description of the book ready to take you directly to the amazon sales page.

I write a lot of books on a wide variety of subjects to cover as large of an audience as possible. I also try to publish at least 13 new books per year. I will write books in series as well. If a series begins to slow down in sales, start adding new volumes to it.

If you want to generate good reviews for your books, simply review my books on amazon, make sure that you put a link to your book in the review, and when I find it, I will follow the link and review your book. This is called a review swap, we can do it as much as you like, I wrote a lot of books, try and catch up! (make sure you click to use the old review page).

When I am promoting a book, I will copy the link from amazon, then I will search face book for pages of related interest, and post my link all over those pages. I have written at least half a dozen recipe books, and there are a lot of face book pages about recipes, cooking, chefs, and more. I will also find news pages on face book to post my books on, the key here is to get your book to go viral on the internet, get it seen and shared by as many persons as possible. My sales are climbing from these very effective marketing tools. My face book community pages are also driving my sales up.

Make sure that you have visited these sites and filled out your profiles and set up your book shelves.

Amazon author page
Shelfari
Pinterest
Good reads
Face book community pages
Wikia
Myspace
Linkdin
Twitter
Flickr
Youtube.

Make a video book trailer and upload it to youtube, face book, and your website. If you do not have a website I recommend Yola.

Yahoo is my home page, my yahoo profile picture is one of my book titles, the words attached to it are a keyword phrase related to alchemy since I have published an entire series of books and videos on this subject. I like to look through the news articles posted on my home page and I will frequently comment on them which leaves my book information posted all over the web. I can switch to Aol and do the same thing over there. If you publish a book at create space, you will have a create space sales page for each book. There is a link for this page which you can share all over the internet. In your member dashboard you will see the set of numbers by your title. Just add those numbers to the end of this www.createspace.com/ Here is an example of one of my books,

www.createspace.com/4195395 this book (casino survival guide), contains a really good roulette strategy that you can use to have fun and win money, it took me many years to learn this from experience and studying the game.

You can type your links all over the place, post pictures of your books on Flickr and type the create space links in the comments section. Here is a very popular new recipe book, this book is selling like hotcakes, it is called the kitchen ninja and it is part of a series.

www.createspace.com/4458243 The Kitchen Ninja
and here is the second edition of this book, www.createspace.com/4479668

Realize that by creating and distributing this book, I am creating the potential to increase the reviews and sales of my other books, I could pay for some type of book promotion which would more than likely cost more than it is worth, or I can create a 99 cent ebook which will actually be more effective.

I am on twitter, my screen name is stevealex3, follow me if you like. If I see another author tweeting his or her books I will most definitely retweet your books to my followers, as well as share to facebook, post to my pinterest page, swap amazon, good reads, and barnes and noble reviews. I would appreciate if you do the same for me, good karma.

There are people who prefer an ebook, there are some who prefer a printed book, there are others who would rather have and audio book, or a dvd, or an mp3, or an instant video download. So try to offer products in as many of these different formats as you can. And think about using a keyword phrase as your title, use a key word phrase that is directly related to your subject matter, and this will boost your sales. Make sure that you put a lot of thought into your cover, description, title, and keywords. It is how you get your book seen, and purchased.

Create space is very easy to work with, they have the free option and the paid option if you would like professional assistance creating your masterpiece. I choose the free options because they are so simple and easy to follow, although if you wanted a really exceptional, professional quality book cover, then you might try getting assistance with that. I myself am happy with the free book covers that I create with their cover creator program. Once I download the formatted template and complete my book, I simply click on the cover creator program and design my book cover, and my book is ready to submit for review. At this stage I can also upload it to Nook and Kobo directly from my computer. Once the create space review process is complete, I can publish my product on create space, amazon, and kindle. Uploading it to Nook and Kobo has shown a huge increase in my sales. The point is to get your product listed for sale at as many places on the internet as possible. It is great publicity, and it is free. One thing that I really like about kindle is that amazon is worldwide, amazon.uk, amazon.in, et cetera, and all of those places are selling my electronic books.

On face book I can create a community page for each book that I publish, I can link them all together by logging in as one page and then liking all the other pages I have created as well as sharing things back and forth from one page to the other and inviting all of the people on my friends list to come and like the page, share the page, or share the books that are posted there, as well as post their own books. You can post your books all over my face book pages and I will be happy to promote them for you. When I create a face book page for one of my books, I will post all of my books on each one of those pages with plenty of links to their sales pages from amazon, create space, and barnes and noble.

On Flickr, I will choose one of my products at a time, I will spend two or three days researching keywords, and keyword phrases, and I will collect several pages of these. I will then upload my book cover picture to Flickr, I will attach about two paragraphs worth of keywords to it and click upload, I will then post the sales page link in the comments section of the photo, then I will re post another copy of the same book cover photo, but with a whole new batch of key words, I will do this until I have used all of the words and phrases that I came up with. When I begin typing a keyword into Flickr, it will also generate key words, therefore I will also take advantage of this and use all of these as well.

When I create a video book trailer and upload it to youtube, I will scroll down to the comments section under the video and post keywords there as well. These comments will be seen by the search engines. I track my book promotions, when I am doing this, I will pick one single book to promote for the day, and I will formulate a specific plan to get this book selling, for example, I go to Amazon and look up my book, the first thing I do when I get there is use the twitter, pinterest, and face book icons to share my book. Then I click the share icon and copy the link, now I go to face book and search by key word for all of the news groups and post my book all over those pages, over the next twenty four hours I will log in to my create space member dash board to check my sales and see what effect that this strategy had on my sales figures, and in this way I know which strategies work, and how effective each particular strategy is. Generally when I create a book, I will do all of my promotional techniques right then and there and then move on to another project. If I notice that I have had a day of no sales, (which is highly unusual), then I will go through my books and start promoting them again, which may include creating an ebook or youtube video as well as every other method that I have listed in this book. This book is a gold mine for publicity, you can create your own book similar to this one and include a list of authors that will do review swaps, add me to the list. All you have to do is explain that the reviewer needs to simply review a book from the list, and include a link to their book in the review, and that when the review is found by the books author they will follow the link and review the other persons book.

Here is an experiment, I would like to see how many amazon review swaps that I can generate for these three books in one year's time. I will set the start date at 1-1-2014, I will see how many reviews accrued by 1-1-2015
Make sure you put a link to your book in the review, the very instant that I find it, I will begin reviewing your book. If I haven't reviewed your book, it simply means that I haven't seen the review yet, but I will definitely get there, and I am usually prompt. (The fastest way to swap reviews is to purchase each other's E book and read it).

Here is book number one, The Kitchen Ninja 2, by Steven School.
http://amzn.com/B00FVURRNM

Here is book number two, Alchemy And The Green Lion, the truth of the philosophers stone, by Steven School.
http://amzn.com/1481028456

Here is book number three, Chinese Takeout Recipes by Steven School.
http://amzn.com/B00F7GRZCI

As I have explained before, both the reviews and the links in this system will increase your book sales, as well as mine, because all of those people who are reading my book reviews will see your book, and vice versa. The more good reviews that our books have, the more inclined the customer will be to make a purchase. The minimum goal that I would like to achieve is thirty reviews for each one of my books. If I get three hundred good reviews I will sell a lot more, but at thirty reviews I will already generate plenty of sales.

Every single time that I look up one of my books on an online sales platform, I will use all of the social media icons to promote and share my book, no matter how often it is. The more you promote your work, the more it will sell.

When I publish a book at create space, at the end of the process are the sales channels. There is standard distribution and expanded distribution. When I first began publishing with this platform, the standard distribution was free, and the expanded distribution was costing twenty five dollars per book. I tried it on two of my books to see how it would work. Then shortly thereafter when I logged into create space, I noticed that they had unlocked the expanded distribution and that it was free, this was a gold mine!, I very quickly put the expanded distribution on every single one of my books, and soon after I did, I noticed my books were advertised all over the place, they are on web sites that I never even heard of, they were suddenly on ebay and in the Barnes and noble computer as well as a myriad of other places, this was very exciting news for me and it also motivated me to get back in the game and start publishing more books. I originally intended for this book to be an electronic book only, but I do want to utilize the expanded distribution resource and for that reason alone I will need to offer a printed version of this book. It is too valuable of a resource to pass up, and create space is the only self publishing platform that I have found, which has this feature.

Another valuable resource is windows live movie maker, I bought a new lap top for close to nine hundred dollars in 2011, I had never heard of this program but found it by accident in my computer in 2013 which was after I had already published at least sixteen books. Soon after I had begun learning how to use this program it was so exciting that I began making youtube video book trailers, as well as promotional videos to put on face book and various web sites, which in turn generated a lot of publicity and a ton of sales. I also used the program to begin creating DVD's and publishing them. Of course I made promotional videos on youtube to promote the DVD's as well.

Here is my first DVD.
www.createspace.com/381734
 I generated a lot of sales for this item simply by creating the promotional video on youtube, and then sharing the promo video to my own face book page, as well as searching face book by keyword to find the alchemy related pages and posting it there as well. I have already generated hundreds of books sales through face book, and I am just getting warmed up, face book has a lot to offer for those who are interested in promoting a book. You have the potential to sell millions of copies of your book on that one web site alone. Make full use of it.

The magnum opus DVD.

www.createspace.com/381734

Here is a second dvd that I am working on publishing and will be available soon. It was created with windows live movie maker and is being published through create space. Another addition to my portfolio of publications which I consider to be better than a 401K.

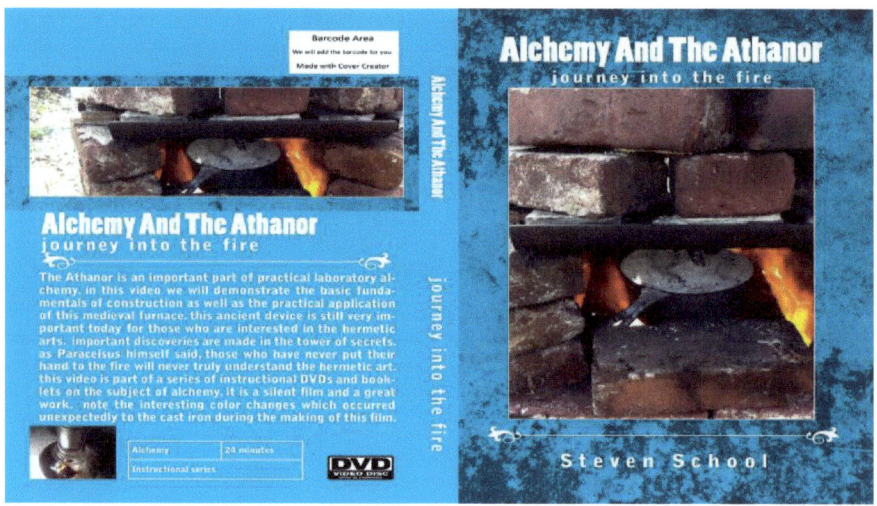

www.createspace.com/388897

Here is my master piece that I am working on.

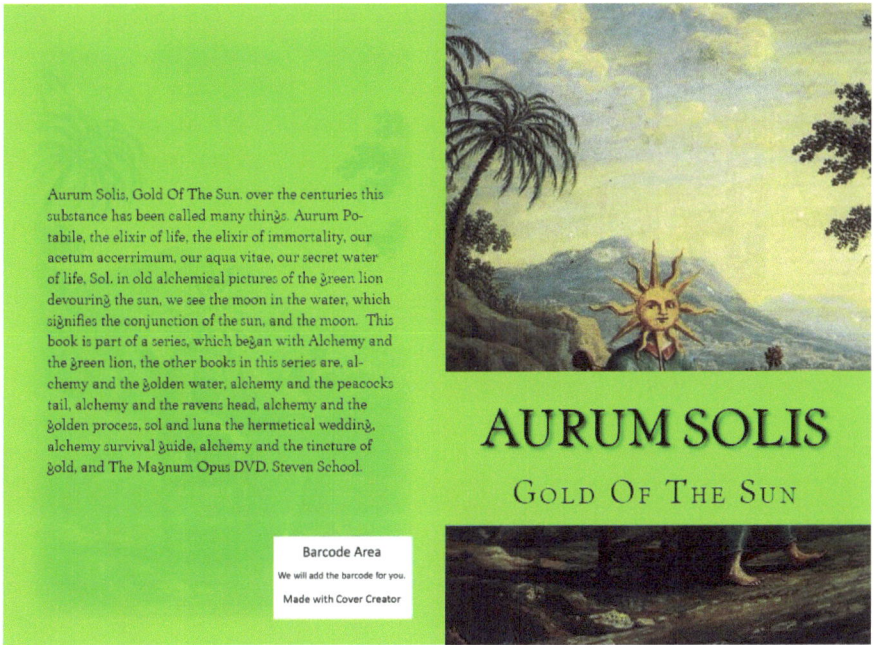

www.createspace.com/4461027

This book is part of my alchemy series which contain an assortment of printed books, electronic books, and DVD's. notice on the back cover that each edition promotes all of the others in the series. At some point in the future I will add an audio book and an instant video download to this series, I have received requests for both so there definitely is a market for it. All of my covers were created by me, at create space, using the free cover creator program.

In my youtube video's I have placed both key words and key word phrases. I have placed them directly into the title, I may actually use a key word phrase as the title and make the video a collage or slide show of words and pictures featuring several or all of my books, I may sometimes set the video to music, or leave it as a silent film. I place key words and phrases in the description of the video before uploading it, as well as in the actual tag section which is reserved for adding keywords. All of these things will increase my rank in the search results, the bottom line is that these tips will get more people to see my promotional videos and that means more sales at the end of the day. Don't forget to click the share button under your video on youtube and make use of all those social media sites that pop up to share your work.

I also put keywords and phrases inside my internet video's, the search engines can see the content of my video, so by using the caption tool in windows movie maker, I can add a picture of my book cover, and then add a key word or phrase on to the picture. I can and will use the credit section at the end of the video to insert a myriad of key word phrases which are much more effective than a single key word, however I like to use a mixture of both.

In the older days of telephone book advertising companies used to design their advertisement around the fact that the books were in alphabetical order, this is why we see company names like AAA pool supply. So I will use this technique still, just in case it is still effective anywhere in today's modern marketing system.

I might make a web page to promote a book, and either in the title, description, key word section, or all of the above, put something like, alchemy, alchemy, how to make the philosophers stone. I should try aardvark alchemy and design a free web page on face book as well as one on wikia and use this title, then list all of my alchemy products with links and descriptions as well as all of my other books. If you find aardvark alchemy on face book, feel free to post your books on my page, I have well over one thousand people on my friends list, I am working on building that number up to five thousand, and I will share your book with all of them including my network of authors who work together to promote each other's work. We all share, tweet and repin each other's work all the time. So far I have built up a handful of authors in my network but I would like to have three dozen to maximize effectiveness. I have three twitter accounts of my own, not counting my author network, and I will tweet your book to all of my followers if you will tweet mine!

I like the word integrity, I like to work with honest people who keep their word, mean what they say, and have good intentions. I myself am very highly motivated to promote my work. I like to network with other authors who are also highly motivated to get on the ball and get something done. When an author sends me a request for a review swap, normally I will immediately start reading their work give them a review, after all that is what we want isn't it?, good reviews and promptness. But by the same token, you can bet that I will repeatedly be checking my reviews to see if the favor was returned because I want my goodie too, just like your pet wants its treat. Well as the days go by and the author hasn't bothered to post my review, I am not happy. I start to think that this person is self centered and might not care about anyone but themselves and their own work. By the time a week goes by of being ignored I will be flat unhappy. You can bet that after a month of this I will be deleting reviews and not including that author in any more networking or promotional endeavors. I know that you want a good review on your book, it is exciting to see and you are probably eager for it to occur as soon as possible. So when it is my turn to review your book I will do it as soon as I become aware of it, and I am no different, I want the same thing on my book. When you pull into the drive through with a car load of hungry people do you want to discover that it is going to take them twenty minutes to prepare your order?, I want prompt service. I have done review swap agreements with some authors who never kept their end of the bargain. Some of them actually posted comments in promotional forums later, wondering why some of their five star reviews had been deleted, Gee go figure. The bottom line is, working together we can accomplish a lot more than we can by ourselves, but if you do not care about me or my product, then don't expect me to care about yours. As a result of this, I no longer give my review until after I have received mine. Just today I had to go on amazon and good reads and delete reviews. Someone messaged me recently asking to do a review swap, as soon as I received the message I went directly online and got to work on their review, then the person sent me another message saying that they wanted a review on good reads, I promptly gave the review, then I looked up the authors face book promotional page, let them know that their reviews were done, and asked them to return the favor. Days went by, I posted a reminder, they said oh yeah, I will get it done pretty soon. Another day went by, and I figured there is just no point waiting any longer, it is time to delete the good reviews that I gave them and boot them out of my network. I do not want any flakes, self centered persons, or people with no integrity in my network. I want to be the world's next huge success story, and I want to network with other people of the same mindset. I am not interested in waiting for a slow poke to get off the couch, I want to be able to rely on my people. So that when we start promoting each other's work, it is like firing up a giant machine and things instantly start happening. Reviews are adding up right now, books are going viral because they are being shared and posted all over the world, sales are skyrocketing into the millions this month, not hoping that it might occur ten years from now. I have four basic strategies for accomplishing my goal, which is millions of sales. Here they are,

Step number one, publish as many products as possible.

Step number two, give the customer variety so that I can reach the largest audience possible, this means variety in subject matter, I have books on gambling, cooking, karate, dating, science, and more. Variety in price, I have products from 99 cents on up to $26.95. variety in format, I have electronic books, printed books, DVD's, and I will be adding mp3's, audio cd books, and instant video downloads in the future.

Step number three. Promote my books. The number one person that you can rely on is yourself, the more you promote your work the more it will sell. You could hire a book promoter, he will quote a price, you will write the check, he will go to the bank, then he will go to lunch, then he might think about going out and buying something with the money that you have just thrown in the toilet. Meanwhile you might be wondering why your books are not selling and what this person is actually doing for you, and now you know. His goal was to get your money, and now that his task is complete, he no longer cares about you or your book unless you throw more money at him a second time, and go through the same exact process again, still wondering why your books are not selling even though you have thrown ten grand in the toilet. With sales people their goal is all the same, only the product or service is different, they all will tell you whatever you need to hear to get your money and then disappear out of sight. The bottom line is that it is you who needs to promote your book, and when you realize that most of it is free, a little bit of it is very cheap, and none of it needs to be expensive, you might wonder about the publishers and book promoters that are asking for thousands of dollars to promote your book. They don't get results for us, we get results for us.

Step number four. Build a network of motivated authors who are eager to work together to promote each other's products to generate millions of sales right now, not next week or next month or next year. When your baby wants food, he wants it now, or he will throw a big temper tantrum, and we are all just big kids. My motivation gets results fast in my sales reports, and as with all things, what i get out of it, is based on what I put into it. If you enroll in a karate class you cannot just sit and watch from the sidelines and expect to earn a black belt, you have to get up, get motivated, participate, start networking with the others in the class, and get it done. It is no different with book sales, if you just write a book or two, and then go back to the couch and the bag of potato chips, then you reap what you sow. I want to simply fire up the machine and get instant results. Millions of dollars now. That is what motivation brings in book promotion. There are books out there now that have sold nearly one hundred million copies, how would you like to be the author that wrote that book?, do you think the sales just magically occurred?, or do you think the author is motivated to promote his work and that he has a network of highly motivated people all working together?

I know one author who published his first book. Right out of the gate he was selling bulk orders and his book sales were more than five hundred copies per week, yet there really is nothing special, or intriguing about this man, or his book. His book sales continue to climb, it is network and motivation, that is all that it is. He is now bragging about all that money from his sales, and dreaming about what he will do with the funds. In his network, things happen now, the book is written, and then the machine is turned on and the rocket ship blasts off into outer space, it does not fizzle out on the launch pad with scientists scrambling around looking like clowns.

Swap reviews, share, tweet, repin, work together, get up, and get motivated, do it now, not next week or next year.

Are you wondering what my sales reports look like?, what sales figures I am getting?, do you think that they occurred by accident?, or stroke of luck?
The world meets no one half way, if you want it, you have to make it happen. I have read reports of other authors giving advice to new authors and saying that if you are getting any book sales at all that you are doing really good, these types of pep talks are ridiculous and pathetic. I have given you the tools, now it is up to you to get motivated and empower yourself to rise up into the ranks of the world's bestselling authors.

If I promote your work, I am promoting my own work because people who are interested in your book will take notice of me since I am the one who put your work in front of their face, and therefore they now see and take notice of my work, if you return the gesture and the whole thing goes round and round through our author network all sharing, tweeting, reviewing, and repinning each other's work then it goes viral, the rocket ship takes off, we have ignition, and our sales reports blast off into the next millennium. Fire up the machine!

I published my first book about 14 months ago, now I have twenty books published (not counting this one), and two DVD'S that says something about the kind of motivation that I have, I also have more than forty promotional videos on youtube and posted all over the web. I have dozens of promotional pages and web sites for my work. I have thousands upon thousands of links posted online which will take you directly to my sales pages where you can simply click and buy. I have accomplished a tremendous amount in fourteen months. I remember first starting out with no sales in the first few months, I got motivated and started researching online how to improve my sales, I watched it climb, shortly after I was excited to see my first five hundred dollar month in book sales, and looking back as we head into the new year, how small that five hundred dollar month looks now. Are you one of those authors who only want to review certain types of books?, in a review swap do you order the other persons book, wait for it to arrive, or download the ebook, then sit and read it word for word, spending a week contemplating the information before creating a detailed review?, if you are that is fine. I want millions of sales, right now, the very instant that I see someone has left me a five star review with a link to their book, I will immediately return the favor. It is that simple. The bottom line is we want good reviews now, and millions of sales now. I could order your printed book and wait for it in the mail, working at a snails pace and getting nothing done, or I can fire up my network machine and watch the sales blast off now. Why do I want a good review on my book?, do I simply just like collecting reviews, like making a scrapbook of newspaper clippings?, NO. I want big sales, and I want them now. Not after the economy gets worse, or the dollar crashes, or the countries credit rating goes down another notch. Even if the economy is bad here, or in other countries, my books are available for sale all over the world, so if sales are low in one country, chances are that they are high in several others. Do you want big sales now?, let's get the ball rolling. I would like to network with authors who have goals, my minimum goal is to get one million book sales, hopefully much more, but I will not accept less. Do you want to be in the million sales club?, if you are ok with just getting ten thousand sales then we are probably not compatible to network together because, I want to swim with the big fish. If you think that you deserve to be in the million sales club, if you think you have what it takes, motivation and integrity, then look me up on face book and send a friend request, Steve School. You will see a picture of a book cover as my profile picture. You can look through my community pages which are all linked together, start posting your books on all of my pages, start sharing all of my books, start reviewing tweeting and pinning my products as well as your own, I will do the same for you, interact with the other authors on my friends list and together we will fire up the machine.

This is a very popular book, it is part of a series and I am currently writing the third volume, I will write a dozen books all at the same time.

www.createspace.com/4458243

I am writing more than a dozen books right now, I have decided to finish this book, Tools of The Trade first, and then I will begin knocking out all the others, I also am continually beginning new books so that I always have at least half a dozen books in various stages. This way on any day that I desire I can choose one book, get motivated, and finish publishing it. Hey!, who is that handsome guy in the top left corner?

Here is another book that I wrote, this one is very popular and generates a lot of sales.

www.createspace.com/4277071

My casino book, if you sometimes gamble, try the roulette strategy. Merry Christmas.

www.createspace.com/4195395

I have already mentioned that when I write a book, I list my other titles somewhere near the last page, so that each book promotes the others. The same is true with my series of instructional DVD's, at the end of each movie you will see a slide show presentation of my other products. When I am promoting one of my DVD's, I will create a printed book and an electronic book specifically to help promote the DVD. Now all three of these items are selling and promoting each other, and I am getting paid to promote my work, instead of paying for publicity. I cannot put expanded distribution on my DVD, but I can create a printed book to promote it, I can put expanded distribution on the printed book, I can then offer this book in electronic format so that I can list it on kindle, Nook, kobo, smash words, ibooks, and a few other platforms, all increasing my publicity and bringing attention back to my DVD.

To promote a book, create another book!, the most successful books are written in series. A series will do so much more than a single book will do, although I do like to have a few singles out there as well, but I have two series that I continue to add new volumes to and those generate the largest sales, as well as get the most publicity. I am expanding my portfolio into science fiction, mystery thrillers, and romance novels, but Rome was not built in a day, a good novel takes about nine months to two years to write. It should become either a trilogy or a series. It should be available in printed version, electronic book, and audio book on cd. All of these things will help to optimize sales and publicity.

Any person who purchases a book from one of my series, and likes the book, is likely to purchase the whole series as well as creating word of mouth advertising by telling their friends and by sharing on face book.

A series of books is never finished, I will start a series, publish a few or several books in it, then I will put it down for awhile and work on other projects. At any given time in the future, as new ideas occur to me, I can always come back and publish new additions.

On all of my internet profiles such as Yahoo, Aol and Google, I post a picture of one of my book covers as my profile picture, I may even list the book title in the name section, or a related keyword phrase about my subject matter. Now as I surf the internet posting comments on various new articles or on other people video's, everywhere that I go, I am promoting my book, and it in turn will promote the whole assortment of other products that I have created.

When I come across news articles I will find the comments, even if I have nothing to say I will post something like cool, interesting, or happy holidays, just so that my book is posted there for all to see.

The more active I am online, the more publicity and sales I get, I treat face book the same way, if I see that a post is generating a lot of comments, I will join the discussion just to post my avatar of my book cover for everyone to see. I will also post my books and try to get others to share them. I have sales occurring even as I am writing this book. By posting comments, I can actually use keywords in the statements, which can be found in search results. Like posting on youtube video's for example. Your comments on video's there can be seen by the search engines. Find all of the social media sites that you can, and fill out a free page for all of your books, on face book community pages, make sure that your page is set to public, otherwise it will be blocked from the search engines.

The information that I am sharing with you in this book, has already caused me to get thousands of sales which I would otherwise not have recieved. By the time that you are reading this book, that number will probably have climbed into the tens of thousands, by the time the readers of this book actually get motivated and start networking with me, my sales should be in the hundreds of thousands, the sooner that you get motivated to jump aboard, the sooner you can start catching up. I will watch my sales climb into the millions, while some others sit on the couch and wonder why can't I be like him? Why is my book not selling a million copies? I have my bag of potato chips and my couch here, I am waiting patiently for a sale to come along, but there are none! Check out my website, share it with others.

http://www.howtomakethephilosophersstone.com

If this book is promoting my other products, as well as generating book reviews and publicity for me, should I be happy earning 35 to 45 cents per sale on this book?, I AM.

Here are some ideas to get you rolling in book promotion, I have already been utilizing these methods and still do it all the time, scouring the internet to make sure that I have left no stone unturned.

Your favorite search engine, a powerful tool at your fingertips.
Start searching phrases like how to publish a book, how to publish an ebook, self publishing platform, book marketing strategies, how to promote a book, how to increase book sales, what types of books sell the most? And similar phrases, just look at the wealth of information that comes up, I advise you to choose the free options.

There is one thing that I would like to say, I have made it clear that the goal is sales, reviews are part of the process, if we did a review swap on amazon, let us say that I go there and put five star reviews on two of your books, then you in turn look up one of my books, and give it a review. Does this sound fair?, should I be happy?, I worked very hard to generate reviews and was jipped out of one, if for some reason you do not see the logic, or simply do not care, for whatever reason, then don't be surprised when eventually I go back and delete something. You get back what you put into it, so if you do not care about promoting my books, then I also do not care about promoting yours. I periodically will go through and clean up the mess. I gave good reviews to well over a hundred other authors on amazon, out of all those people, only three of them returned the favor. even though those reviews increase my sales because I put links to my books in them, eventually I will go back and delete the ones that were not returned, simply because those persons do not deserve my reviews and links helping to promote their products.

When you are posting key words on your videos and web sites, Google the subject that your product is about. At the bottom of the search results page you will see "related searches", use this to determine more key word phrases that might fit your product. Another thing to remember is that a keyword phrase will do much better in search results than a single keyword. I recently typed the word alchemy into a search engine and realized that there were something like 13,500,000 search results. So my product that used this keyword had no hope of even showing up in this mess, and we really need to be on the first page of search results if we can, or at least in the first few pages.

Using keyword phrases really picked up my visibility and my sales soon followed. I published my first series which was on the ancient hermetic science of alchemy. I realized as I was creating and promoting this series that as I added new titles, I could research keyword phrases related to alchemy and use this information to design the titles and subtitles of my books, this dramatically increased my visibility in search results.

The information that I have shared with you in this book, has done wonders for my book sales, and now it is your turn. Decide who you want to be, and let's get to work.

Other Books I Have Written.

Alchemy and the green lion
Alchemy and the golden water
Alchemy and the peacocks tail
Alchemy and the ravens head
Alchemy and the golden process
Alchemy and the tincture of gold
Sol and Luna the hermetical wedding
Alchemy survival guide
The Magnum Opus DVD.
Alchemy And The Athanor DVD.
Casino survival guide breaking the bank
Chinese takeout recipes
How to make money
Karate secrets revealed
The kitchen ninja
The kitchen ninja 2
Grandmas delicious recipes
The secret recipe book
Trophy wife
Booze survival guide
Wilderness survival tips
Kitchen survival guide

And much more coming in 2014 such as Aurum Solis, Gold of the Sun.

Checkout youtube video titled alchemy, aquarius, alembic, aludel, distillation.

ABOUT THE AUTHOR

    I enjoy cooking at home from scratch, I like writing and have been interested in becoming an author for many years, thanks to amazon my dream has become a reality. I enjoy the company of my Rottweilers, I also enjoy the hermetic arts and have been studying alchemy diligently since 2008 with an emphasis on the white and red philosophers stones, the elixir of life, and the primum ens mellisa.
    I was born in the winter of 1969.

www.ingramcontent.com/pod-product-compliance
Lightning Source LLC
Chambersburg PA
CBHW041146180526
45159CB00002BB/741